J.J. Wiggins

Copyright © 2017 by J.J. Wiggins

All rights reserved.

No part of this book may be reproduced, stored in a retrieval system, or transmitted in any form or by any means, electronic, mechanical, photocopying, recording, or otherwise, without the prior written permission of the copyright owner.

Edition: 1.0

"There is nothing in the world so irresistibly contagious as laughter and good humor."

— Charles Dickens

Contents

1. **Holiday Jokes**......................7

2. **People & Things**.................22

3. **Science & Technology**.....36

4. **Around The World**............50

5. **Plants & Animals**...............66

6. **Food & Entertainment**....84

7. **Glossary Of Fun Facts**...100

Holiday Jokes

Who haunts the Christmas tree every year?

The Ghost of Christmas Presents!

MY FAVORITE JOKES

What do elves learn in kindergarten?

The Elf-abet.

What do elves like to do on vacation?

Take elfies!

Where do children get presents all year round?

On Christmas Island.

__Fun Fact:__ Christmas Island is a real place! It's located in the Indian Ocean and home to over 2000 people.

Where do deer go for coffee?

To Star-bucks!

What do snowmen have for breakfast?

Frosted Snowflakes!

What is Santa's favorite kind of chips?

Kris Pringles.

__Fun Fact:__ Pringles are sold in more than 140 countries around the world!

What is Frosty's least favorite drink?

Hot chocolate!

What did Frosty say to the children he met?

"Ice to meet you!"

Why is Rudolph's nose so red?

Because he has the sniffles.

Why doesn't Rudolph like the sun?

Because he's a rain-deer! (reindeer)

What do mothers sing to their newborn on Christmas Eve?

"Silent Night," cause they need one!

What is Aunt Liz's favorite Christmas song?

Fe-liz Navidad!

Which Christmas Carol does Old Man Winter like most?

"Let It Snow! Let It Snow! Let It Snow!"

What do squirrels like to watch at the theater?

"The Nutcracker."

<u>Fun Fact:</u> This ballet was first performed a week before Christmas in 1982.

Where can Santa and his elves go dancing?

At the "Snow Ball."

MY FAVORITE JOKES

Where was the little piggy born?

In Bethle-ham!

What did one cat say to the other on December 25?

"Meow-y Christmas!"

Why didn't Sally want to kiss Johnny?

Because he had smelly mistle-toes.

Why did the butcher throw the zombie in the trash?

Because it was dead meat.

What do zombies get at the hair salon?

Dreadlocks.

What did the mummy do for Christmas?

He wrapped himself up!

What did the cat dress up as for Halloween?

Santa Claws.

What do birds like to do on Halloween?

Go twick-or-tweeting.

Which game do ghosts play on Easter?

Scavenger Haunt!

What do ghosts like to do in winter?

Go to-boo-ganning!

Why wasn't the turkey at Thanksgiving dinner?

Because it was already stuffed.

Fun Fact: *People from Canada celebrate Thanksgiving in October, while people from the United States celebrate it in November!*

Where was the Easter bunny born?

On Easter Island, of course!

Fun Fact: *Easter Island has giant human heads carved out of stone!*

What do witches give on Valentine's Day?

Hugs and curses!

MY FAVORITE JOKES

People & Things

Why did Deedee pinch her nose?

Because her car had gas.

What do you get when you cross a ghost and a tiger?

A booger.

Why are ghosts not allowed to scare little children?

Because it's taboo.

__Fun Fact:__ If something is 'taboo,' it means it's not allowed or unacceptable.

What do you get when you cross a bunny and sticky tape?

Hopscotch. (Scotch tape)

What do old gingerbread men use for walking?

Candy canes.

What did the kitten say when the vet gave it a shot?

"Me, ow!"

What are baby snowmen called?

Freezies.

What game are little clocks good at?

Tick tock toe.

Why was Mark ticked off at his alarm clock?

It wouldn't stop tocking! (talking)

What kind of guns do police bees use?

Bee-bee guns.

PEOPLE & THINGS

Why did Mary scream when she entered the library?

She saw a bunch of bookworms!

__Fun Fact:__ A 'bookworm' is someone who enjoys reading or studying.

MY FAVORITE JOKES

Where do liars learn to lie?

At the lie-brary.

Why didn't the clown get the job?

Because he forgot to put a smile on his face for the interview.

Why couldn't the cat lady speak?

Because the cat's got her tongue.

<u>Fun Fact:</u> 'Cat's got your tongue' just means somebody wants to say something but doesn't know what to say because they can't think.

PEOPLE & THINGS

Why didn't the zookeeper hire the bear from Australia?

Because it wasn't koala-fied for the job! (qualified)

What do you call it when a bunch of apes buy and sell things?

Monkey business.

What did the farmer say to the lazy vegetable?

"Stop being a couch potato!"

Where do monsters park their cars?

In the grrrr-age.

PEOPLE & THINGS

Why did Marvin feel really stupid after going to the dentist?

He had all his wisdom teeth removed.

__Fun Fact:__ Did you know…you don't start growing your wisdom teeth until you're twenty years old!

Why did Grandpa fail the driving exam?

He couldn't read sign language.

Fun Fact: *Sign Language is a way to talk to other people by using your hands. It's used for communicating with deaf people.*

PEOPLE & THINGS

What do you get when you cross a ghost with a former US president?

George Boo-sh. (George Bush)

What do skeletons drive in the winter?

A zam-bone-i! (zamboni)

Fun Fact: A 'zamboni' is a vehicle used to clean and smooth the surface of ice. It was developed in 1949 by a man named Frank Zamboni.

Where do shoes go to become stronger?

To boot-camp.

Why didn't Jimmy feel like playing with his skateboard?

Because he was skate-bored.

PEOPLE & THINGS

What did the teeth say after their appointment with the dentist?

"Thanks, it's very filling!"

__Fun Fact:__ You go to the dentist for a filling when your teeth have cavities. Don't forget to brush your teeth!

Science & Technology

Where can spiders go to order food?

On the web!

<u>Fun Fact:</u> The 'Web' is another word for the Internet. It's called a 'Web' because people from all over the world are connected to each other.

How do birds talk to each other on the Internet?

They tweet!

Where do witches get recipes for their potions?

On Wicca-pedia.

How do leprechauns and rainbows talk to one another?

With Sky-pe.

How do one-eyed monsters do research for their homework?

They use an En-cyclop-edia.

Fun Fact: A 'cyclops' is a giant with one humongous eye in the middle of its forehead!

What do you call a game console falling from a 100-story tall building?

Nintendo Weeeeee!

What game do geniuses play after school?

Mind-craft. (Minecraft)

SCIENCE & TECHNOLOGY

What do you call fake smart phones?

iPhonies.

What do you call an ant that plays with chemicals?

Sci-ant-ist! (scientist)

How did the slime find its way home?

It got directions from Goo-gle!

Fun Fact: *The popular search engine, Google, got its name from the word, googol, which means a number starting with 1, followed by a hundred zeros!*

How do turtles see into space?

They use a shell-escope! (telescope)

What do you call a robot that serves you food and drinks?

A bot-ler. (butler)

What do call a spider that likes to take pictures?

A shutterbug.

What do you call an elephant dancing?

Earthquake!

SCIENCE & TECHNOLOGY

What do you call a robot ant?

An ant-droid. (android)

Fun Fact: An 'android' is a machine that looks and behaves like a human.

What street do cows live on?

Milky Way.

Fun Fact: Did you know...our Earth and sun are found in a galaxy called the Milky Way. The Milky Way has about 200-400 billion stars!

Why was the snowman afraid of the avalanche?

Because it was actually a lava-lanche!

Fun Fact: *Did you know...'lava' is rock that's turned into liquid, and it's very, very hot!*

SCIENCE & TECHNOLOGY

Why did the alien cross the road?

To return to its spaceship before anybody spots it, of course!

What do call a very, very, very, very, small dog?

A fido-plankton. (phytoplankton)

__Fun Fact:__ Amoeba and phytoplankton are very, very small living things that you can only see with a microscope. They live in wet places!

What can you ride that's lighter than a feather?

An air-plane.

Why didn't the moon want any more food?

Because it was already full.

__Fun Fact:__ Did you know...a full moon occurs once about every 27 days.

What sickness do horses get when they eat too much?

Hay fever.

Fun Fact: *Having 'hay fever' means things like dust and pollen make you sneeze and your eyes itchy and watery!*

Why couldn't the horses understand the cows?

The cows were using Moo-rse Code. (Morse code)

Fun Fact: *Morse code is a way to send secret messages to other people using clicking sounds or light.*

Why did the cat jump on the computer?

Because it saw a mouse.

SCIENCE & TECHNOLOGY

What do you call a pie flying through the air at 600 mph?

A pie-lot. (pilot)

Fun Fact: Did you know...the record for the fastest flight speed is over 2000 mph, more than 3 times the speed of sound!

Where do alien ants come from?

Ant-dromeda. (Andromeda)

Fun Fact: Andromeda is the closest galaxy to the Milky Way at about 2.2 million light years away!

Around The World

What do insects use to find accommodations when they travel?

AirBee-n-Bee!

How do French people say 'I love you' when they're in England?

"Je Thames!"

Fun Fact: *The correct way to say 'I love you' in French is 'Je t'aime.'*

What do you call a Roman alligator holding a sword?

gladi-gator! (gladiator)

What is a slime's favorite type of drink?

Ouzo.

Where do beavers go for vacation?

To Amster-dam!

Fun Fact: *Did you know...Amsterdam is in the Netherlands, a country in Europe.*

What did the sheep have for dinner?

Baa-baa ganoush. (baba ganoush)

What did the sheep have for dessert?

Baa-klava. (baklava)

__Fun Fact:__ Baklava is a pastry from the Middle East filled with nuts and honey. Yummy!

Where do cute little birds come from?

The Canary Islands.

Which country probably doesn't like visitors very much?

No-way. (Norway)

Where should people who can't stop eating food go live?

To Hungary. (hungry)

What did the German shepherd say when he saw his friend?

"Guten Tag!"

Fun Fact: 'Guten Tag' is German and it means 'Hello' or 'Good day.'

Where are electric pokémon found?

On Machu Picchu.

Fun Fact: *Did you know...Machu Picchu is a real place you can visit. It's found high up in the mountains in South America and belonged to the Inca, a civilization that ruled it over 500 years ago!*

What do pigs learn in Language Studies?

Pig Latin.

__Fun Fact:__ Did you know…Pig Latin is a made-up language that you can use to talk to other people in secret!

AROUND THE WORLD

How it works:

1. For words beginning with consonants, move those letters to the end of the word and add '-ay.'

'hello' becomes 'ello-ay'
'plan' becomes 'an-play'

2. For words beginning with vowels, just add '-yay' to the end of the word.

'it' becomes 'it-yay'
'animal' becomes 'animal-yay'

Examples:

Bedroom = Ed-bay oom-ray.
How are you? = Ow-hay are-yay ou-yay?
Good job! = ood-Gay ob-jay!

With these simple rules, you can start speaking to people in code. Of course, they have to know Pig Latin, too. Go teach your friends!

What language does a German Shepherd speak?

Dogs can't talk, silly!

Where do pigs go to relax on the beach?

To Porkto Rico. (Puerto Rico)

AROUND THE WORLD

What do you get when you cross a hummingbird and cheese?

A coli-Brie. (colibri)

Fun Fact: *'Colibri' is another word for hummingbird, and 'Brie' is a type of cheese!*

What do tourist cats do when they're in Egypt?

They visit the Purr-amids. (the Pyramids)

Fun Fact: *There's a giant statue by the pyramids called a 'sphinx', which is a creature that's half-human, half-lion!*

What do you call the baddest sausage in the pack?

The Wurst.

Fun Fact: *'Wurst' is also German, and it means 'sausage.' Would you like one?*

AROUND THE WORLD

Where do cooties come from?

Germ-any!

Which holiday do kitchens in Mexico celebrate?

Sinko de Mayo. (Cinco de Mayo)

Where do king and queen pigs live?

In Bucking-ham Palace.

__Fun Fact:__ Buckingham Palace is found in England, and it's where queens used to live! Today, it's used for special events hosted by the royal family.

In which US states do people always ask a lot of questions?

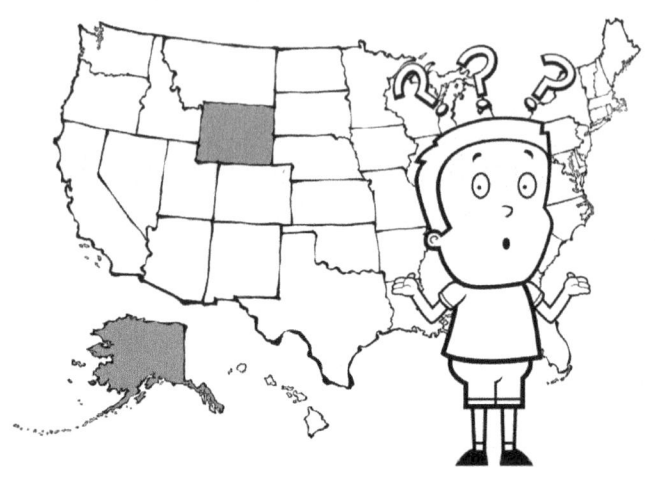

In Why-oming and Al-ask-a.

Where do clowns go for vacation?

To Hahaha-waii. (Hawaii)

Where do vampire trains live?

In Train-sylvania. (Transylvania)

__Fun Fact:__ Did you know…Transylvania is a region in Romania, a country in Europe. It's often seen as a place of magic and mystery, and many vampire movies use it as a setting.

Where do deer come from?

Tim-buck-tu! (Timbuktu)

__Fun Fact:__ Timbuktu is a city in Mali, a country in Africa.

Where do snails go to rent a car?

To Es-car-got. (escargot)

Fun Fact: *'Escargot' is a French word meaning 'snail.'*

What kind of car do dogs drive?

A Furrr-ari. (Ferrari)

What kind of car do sheep drive?

A Lamb-orghini.

What kind of car do Jedis drive?

A To-yoda (Toyota)

Plants & Animals

What do you call a dog with a sombrero?

El Poocho.

What do you get when you cross a blimp and a sheep?

A bleep.

What do you call a kangaroo that works at a hotel?

A bellhop.

Fun Fact: *A bellhop is someone who works at a hotel and helps carry people's bags to their rooms.*

What do you call two vegetables that are very good friends?

Bro-ccolis.

Why didn't the owl do its homework?

Because it didn't give a hoot.

Fun Fact: *'To not give a hoot' means you don't care about something.*

What do you get when you glue two cats together?

An octo-puss.

What do you call two flowers that are best of friends?

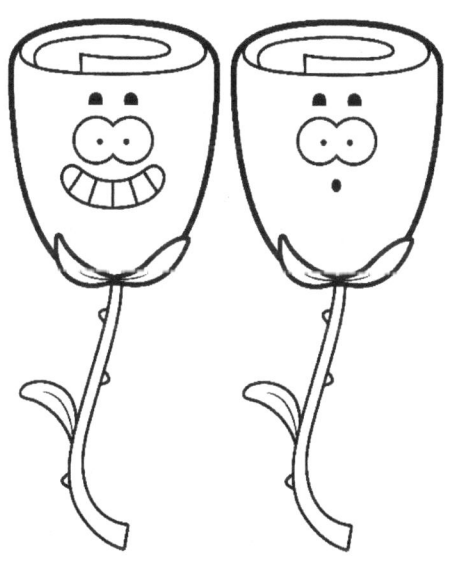

Rose-buds.

What kind of vegetable belongs in the zoo?

A zoo-cchini. (zucchini)

What is a spider's favorite vegetable?

Spin-ach.

Where do pigs put their savings?

In a piggy bank.

How do skunks say goodbye to one another?

"Smell you later."

What is the most beautiful insect in the world?

The ladybug.

What is a dog's favorite vegetable?

Collie-flower.

How do camels hide from dangers in the desert?

By using camel-flage. (camouflage)

Why don't crabs make good friends?

Because they're shellfish! (selfish)

Fun Fact: *'Shellfish' are a type of aquatic animal that has a shell, such as oysters, lobsters, and crabs.*

What's common between fish and music?

They both have scales.

What do you call a mean fish that spread germs?

Barra-cooties. (barracuda)

Why do bees' hairs smell so sweet?

Because they use a honeycomb.

Which insect only appears during one month of the year?

The June bug.

What happened when the snake couldn't catch its prey?

It threw a hissy fit.

What do you get when you cross a pig and a whale?

A porca.

Fun Fact: *Did you know…'orca' is another name for killer whale.*

Where do sheep go for higher education?

To ewe-niversity. (university)

What do you call a snake that's not good at math?

Anything but an adder!

What do vampire bees like to drink after dinner?

Neck-tar. (nectar)

__Fun Fact:__ Nectar is a sweet, sugary liquid that plants produce to attract insects such as bees.

What can you find at a store run by insects?

Flea bargains.

PLANTS & ANIMALS

What do bees do after they get married?

Go on a honeymoon.

What kind of flower is the easiest to remember?

The forget-me-not.

<u>*Fun Fact:*</u> *The forget-me-not is also called 'scorpion grass.'*

What do you call fish that don't belong to you?

Angel fish! (ain't your fish)

What kind of dogs do angels have as pets?

Saint Bernards.

__Fun Fact:__ Saint Bernards are the biggest breed of dog in the world!

What do you call a butterfly that can't fly?

Butter.

Why was the bird scared of the worms?

Because it was chicken!

Why did the mouse break up with her boyfriend?

Because he was too cheesy for her.

What can you find in a church for insects?

Bee-lievers!

Why was the squirrel afraid of the tree?

Because there were too many nuts hanging around.

What do you call a kangaroo that can't hop?

A kan't-garoo!

What do you call a goldfish with no money?

A fish.

What do you call a dog that's really good at football?

A Golden Receiver.

Where do farm animals go when they're not feeling well?

To the duck-tor's!

Food & Entertainment

What do viruses like to watch at the movie theater?

"Star Warts."

What is SpongeBob's sister's name?

SpongeBarb SquarePants.

What movie do silly dwarfs like to watch?

"Snow White and the Seven Doofuses."

__Fun Fact:__ The animated film 'Snow White and the Seven Dwarfs' came out in 1937. That's over 80 years ago!

What is a snowman's favorite animated film?

"Frozen."

What do you call a cooking show about fish?

"Frying Nemo."

What TV show do sloths like to watch?

"American Idle."

FOOD & ENTERTAINMENT

What is a rock's favorite band to listen to?

The Rolling Stones.

Where do stones and pebbles go to enjoy music?

To a rock concert.

What is a sheep's favorite rock band?

Ewe-2. (U2)

__Fun Fact:__ U2 is an Irish rock band that's still very popular today.

Why can't cats ever finish watching a movie?

Because they keep paws-ing it!

What kind of horse can you not ride?

A pommel horse.

What is the most useless exercise to do if you want to lose weight?

Diddly squats.

Which Olympic sport are numbers good at?

Figure skating.

__Fun Fact:__ Figure skating was included in the Winter Olympics in 1908, over 100 years ago!

What exercises are bananas good at?

Splits.

Why didn't the rabbit want to go out and play?

Because it was having a bad hare day.

FOOD & ENTERTAINMENT

What kind of bee can you throw around in the park?

A Frisbee!

What do you get when you mix an assassin with dough and put them in the oven for 45 minutes?

A ninja-bread man.

What do girl bees wear to the beach?

Bee-kinis!

Why couldn't the pig finish the marathon?

Because it tore its ham-string.

Fun Fact: *Your hamstring is the soft part found behind your knees!*

What do spoons and forks play when no one's watching?

Play bowl-ing.

Why couldn't the bread get home?

It was stuck in a peanut butter and traffic jam.

What subject do sodas enjoy most?

Fizz-ed. (Phys-Ed)

Where do numbers go to buy snacks?

To the 7-Eleven.

Why was the mouse sad after breakfast?

Because it had blue cheese.

<u>Fun Fact:</u> *Blue cheese is a very strong type of cheese containing blue mold. It has a very strong smell that most people can't handle!*

What is a skunk's favorite snack?

Mar-shmell-ows. (marshmallows)

What did the squirrel say when he couldn't find his food?

"Ah, nuts!"

MY FAVORITE JOKES

What is the coldest fruit in the world?

The winter melon.

What do sheep like to eat at the amusement park?

Cotton candy.

__Fun Fact:__ Cotton candy is 100% sugar and contains mostly air.

Why didn't the elephants want to go swimming?

Because they forgot their trunks!

What is Dracula's favorite drink?

Bloody Mary.

What happened to the pig that sat in the sun for too long?

It became pork roast.

What do you call a poodle tanning on the beach?

A hot dog!

What is the simplest way to cook an egg?

Over easy.

Fun Fact:* There are many different ways to cook eggs. Hard boiled, soft boiled, sunny side up, poached, scrambled, and over easy.*

Why did the crowd boo the chicken at the soccer game?

Because it was playing fowl ball!

Glossary Of Fun Facts

amoeba: a very small living thing found in water and soil.

Amsterdam: the capital city of the Netherlands, Europe.

android: a machine that looks and behaves like a human.

Andromeda: a galaxy about 2.2 million light years from the Milky Way.

baba ganoush: a dish from the Middle East made with eggplant mixed with onions, tomatoes, olive oil and other seasonings.

baklava: a pastry from the Middle East filled with nuts and honey.

bellhop: someone who works at a hotel and helps carry people's bags to their rooms.

blue cheese: a very strong type of cheese containing blue mold.

bookworm: someone who enjoys reading or studying.

Brie: a kind of cheese made from soft cow's milk, named after a place in France.

Buckingham Palace: a place in England where the royal family works and hosts events.

cat's got your tongue: you don't know what to say.

Christmas Island: an island located in the Indian Ocean and home to over 2000 people.

colibri: another word for hummingbird.

cotton candy: cotton candy is 100% sugar and contains mostly air.

MY FAVORITE JOKES

couch potato: somebody who is very lazy.

cyclops: a giant with one eye in the middle of its forehead.

Easter Island: an island in Polynesian with giant human heads carved out of stone.

escargot: 'snail' in French.

ewe: a female sheep.

figure skating: a sport included in the Winter Olympics in 1908, over 100 years ago.

filling: a treatment you get for cavities at the dentist's.

forget-me-not: a flower with over 70 species. It's also called 'scorpion grass.'

full moon: it occurs once about every 27 days.

GLOSSARY OF FUN FACTS

googol: the number 1 followed by a hundred zeros.

Guten Tag: 'Hello' or 'Good day' in German.

hamstring: the soft part found behind your knees.

hay fever: an allergy caused by dust or pollen.

iPhone: a smart phone made by Apple.

je t'aime: 'I love you' in French.

lava: very hot, liquid rock.

Machu Picchu: a place in South America where the Inca lived.

Milky Way: the galaxy where our solar system and Earth is found.

Morse code: a way to send secret messages using clicking sounds or light.

nectar: a sweet, sugary liquid that plants produce to attract insects such as bees.

orca: another name for killer whale.

phytoplankton: very small living things found in oceans and fresh water bodies.

Pig Latin: a made-up language used by kids to speak in code.

Pringles: a brand of chips sold in more than 140 countries around the world!

Saint Bernard: the biggest breed of dog in the world.

Snow White and the Seven Dwarfs: a Disney animated film which came out in 1937, over 80 years ago.

GLOSSARY OF FUN FACTS

shellfish: a type of aquatic animal that has a shell, such as oysters, lobsters, and crabs.

Sign Language: a way to talk to other people by using your hands.

sphinx: a giant statue by the pyramids of Egypt.

Starbucks: an American coffee shop with over 20,000 locations around the world.

taboo: something unacceptable or not allowed.

Thanksgiving: a holiday celebrated in North America. Canadians celebrate it in October, while Americans celebrate it in November.

The Nutcracker: a ballet first performed in 1982 set to music by Tchaikovsky.

to not give a hoot: to not care about something.

MY FAVORITE JOKES

Timbuktu: a city in Mali, Africa.

Transylvania: a region in Romania, Europe.

U2: an Irish rock band.

Web: another word for the Internet.

wisdom teeth: teeth that you starting growing at around 20 years old.

Wurst: 'sausage' in German.

zamboni: a vehicle used to clean and smooth the surface of ice.

GLOSSARY OF FUN FACTS

Want More?

Get your brain juices flowing
with these puzzle books!

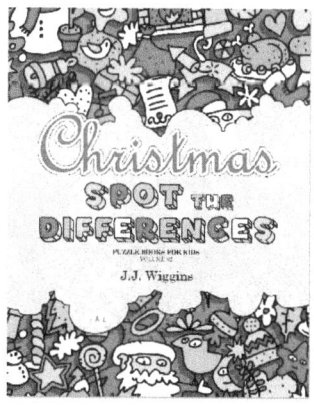

MY FAVORITE JOKES

About The Author

J.J. Wiggins worked in the IT industry where he enjoyed a long and fruitful, yet tedious career. He has since retired and now spends his days with his family, doing his darndest to make them laugh.

http://amazon.com/author/jjwiggins

Thanks for reading!

Made in the USA
Columbia, SC
14 December 2017